GEORGE WASHINGTON

PIVOTAL PRESIDENTS
PROFILES IN LEADERSHIP

GEORGE
WASHINGTON

Edited by Sherman Hollar

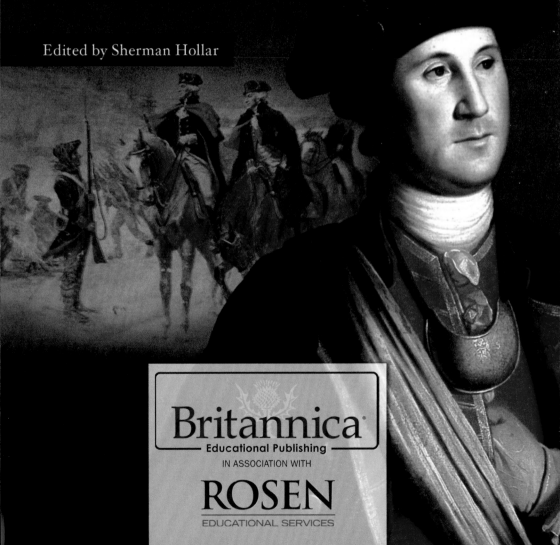

Britannica
Educational Publishing
IN ASSOCIATION WITH
ROSEN
EDUCATIONAL SERVICES

Published in 2013 by Britannica Educational Publishing
(a trademark of Encyclopædia Britannica, Inc.) in association with Rosen Educational Services, LLC
29 East 21st Street, New York, NY 10010.

Distributed exclusively by Rosen Educational Services.
For a listing of additional Britannica Educational Publishing titles, call toll free (800) 237-9932.

First Edition

Britannica Educational Publishing
J.E. Luebering: Director, Core Reference Group, Encyclopædia Britannica
Adam Augustyn: Assistant Manager, Encyclopædia Britannica

Anthony L. Green: Editor, Compton's by Britannica
Michael Anderson: Senior Editor, Compton's by Britannica
Andrea R. Field: Senior Editor, Compton's by Britannica
Sherman Hollar: Senior Editor, Compton's by Britannica

Marilyn L. Barton: Senior Coordinator, Production Control
Steven Bosco: Director, Editorial Technologies
Lisa S. Braucher: Senior Producer and Data Editor
Yvette Charboneau: Senior Copy Editor
Kathy Nakamura: Manager, Media Acquisition

Rosen Educational Services
Jeanne Nagle: Senior Editor
Nelson Sá: Art Director
Cindy Reiman: Photography Manager
Karen Huang: Photo Researcher
Brian Garvey: Designer, Cover Design
Introduction by Jeanne Nagle

Library of Congress Cataloging-in-Publication Data

George Washington/edited by Sherman Hollar. — 1st ed.
  p. cm. — (Pivotal presidents: profiles in leadership)
"In association with Britannica Educational Publishing, Rosen Educational Services."
Includes bibliographical references and index.
ISBN 978-1-61530-939-9 (library binding)
1. Washington, George, 1732-1799 — Juvenile literature. 2. Presidents — United States — Biography —
Juvenile literature. 3. Generals — United States — Biography — Juvenile literature. 4. Leadership —
United States — Case studies — Juvenile literature. I. Hollar, Sherman.
E312.66.G38 2013
973.4'1092 — dc23
[B]

2012015597

Manufactured in the United States of America

On the cover, p. 3 (background image): Detail of painting by John Ward Dunsmore of George
Washington and French officer Marquis de Lafayette (on horseback, left to right) at Valley Forge, Pa.
Library of Congress Prints and Photographs Division

Cover, p. 3: Photos.com/Thinkstock; cover, pp. 1, 3 (flag) © istockphoto.com/spxChrome; pp. 5, 10, 24,
36, 49, 66, 69, 73, 75 Fedorov Oleksiy/Shutterstock.com

Table of Contents

INTRODUCTION

The image of George Washington, carved in stone on the side of Mount Rushmore. Mighty Sequoia Studio/Shutterstock.com

"First in war, first in peace, and first in the hearts of his countrymen." These words were uttered as part of a eulogy for the first president of the United States, George Washington. More than simply a nice speech honoring a public figure who had died, the words revealed a lot about Washington's character. As this book shows, George Washington was indeed a courageous soldier, a respected statesman, and in many ways a true man of the people.

Washington first proved himself a capable military leader somewhat early in life. Joining the military as an assistant officer of a Virginia district at age 20, Washington quickly rose through the ranks and was named commander of all Virginia armed forces within three years. His leadership during the French and Indian War was a big reason why he was made commander in chief of colonial forces at the start of the American Revolutionary War.

During the fight for American independence from Britain, Washington's ability as a military leader seemed to shine the brightest. He led his forces to several victories in New Jersey early in the war, before suffering hard losses in Pennsylvania. Yet even after these defeats and spending a brutal winter in Valley Forge, Washington was able to rally his troops to defeat the British at Yorktown, which was the final battle of the conflict.

In peacetime, following the conclusion of the war, Washington was chosen to preside over the Constitutional Convention, which drafted the new nation's abiding set of laws and rules, the U.S. Constitution. Writing the Constitution was a process that involved many arguments and debates, and required a lot of compromise. As head of the convention, Washington was charged with making sure that discussions didn't get out of hand and leading all parties to the successful completion of their task. The fate of the new nation depended on it.

Once the Constitution was completed, all eyes immediately turned to Washington to serve as the first president of the United States, and he was unanimously elected to the office. Under his political leadership, the country added more states to the Union, established a federal financial system, and adopted the Bill of Rights. Washington set the tone for U.S. foreign relations when he issued the Proclamation of Neutrality in 1793, and showed great diplomacy when settling boundary disputes with Britain and Spain in the years that followed.

In addition to having fame and power, Washington also was a common man. Citizens of the United States could relate to him. He was a family man with a wife and stepchildren. A successful landowner and farmer, Washington frequently got his own hands dirty working in the fields and in his orchards. He was popular with his neighbors. His home at Mount Vernon was the site of many parties and social gatherings.

Washington was well-known for being a military and political leader. He was also a working man and a gracious host. These traits have combined to make Washington a beloved figure in his time and for all time.

CHAPTER 1

Early Life and Career

George Washington occupies a pre-eminent place among the heroes of American history. As a military leader, he guided the colonial forces to victory against Great Britain in the American Revolution. After the war he was a delegate to and presiding officer of the Constitutional Convention and helped secure ratification of the United States Constitution. When the state electors met to select the first president, Washington was the unanimous choice, and in his eight years as president (1789–97), he did much to establish a strong central government.

Before becoming the Father of His Country, as he is often called, Washington was a young boy growing up on plantations and a farm in Virginia.

CHILDHOOD AND YOUTH

In 1657 John Washington, George Washington's great-grandfather, came to Virginia from England. John obtained a grant of 150 acres (61 hectares) in Westmoreland County on the Potomac River. He soon saw a future in the wilderness upriver. In 1674 John secured a second grant of 5,000 acres

The first president was born at the Wakefield estate in Virginia. It is now George Washington Birthplace National Monument. **National Park Service**

(2,023 hectares) about 15 miles (24 kilometers) south of modern-day Washington, D.C., where he established the Wakefield plantation for his family.

John's grandson, Augustine Washington, also was a prosperous landowner. Augustine managed farms, businesses, and mines. Augustine added to the Wakefield plantation until it included the entire peninsula between Popes Creek and Bridges Creek, small streams emptying into the Potomac River.

Augustine's first wife died in 1730, and the following year he married Mary Ball. Their first child, George Washington, was born on Feb. 22 (Feb. 11 on the calendar used then), 1732, on the Wakefield plantation in Westmoreland County, Va. The couple had five more children—Elizabeth, Samuel, John Augustine, Charles, and Mildred (who died in infancy). George also had two older half brothers, Lawrence and Augustine, children from Augustine's first marriage.

In 1735 the Washington family moved farther up the Potomac River to the Epsewasson (Little Hunting Creek) plantation, named after the stream it faced. A few years later they moved to Ferry Farm on the Rappahannock River, opposite Fredericksburg, Va. Ferry Farm

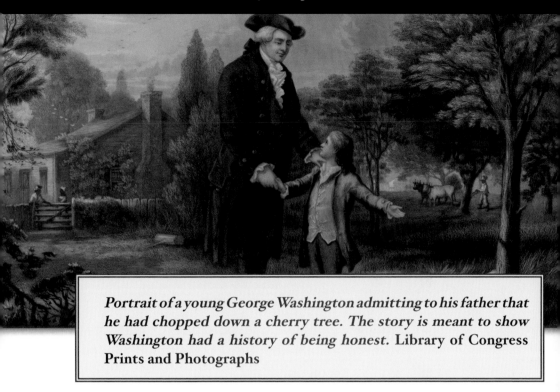

Portrait of a young George Washington admitting to his father that he had chopped down a cherry tree. The story is meant to show Washington had a history of being honest. **Library of Congress Prints and Photographs**

was the setting of George's boyhood adventures described by Mason Locke Weems in his book *The Life and Memorable Actions of George Washington* (1800). According to Weems, George chopped down a cherry tree with a hatchet and later admitted it to his father, stating that he could not tell a lie. Weems also related how George threw a stone across the Rappahannock River, but it is unknown whether or not these stories are based on facts.

George's father died in 1743, and his property was divided among his nearest heirs.

Mount Vernon

One of the most beautiful historic sites in the United States is Mount Vernon, the estate and burial place of George Washington. The stately mansion is on a high bluff overlooking the Potomac River 15 miles (24 kilometers) south of Washington, D.C.

The Mount Vernon site became a Washington family possession in 1674. Washington's father took possession of the property in 1726 and moved his family there in 1735. They moved again in 1739, and the property passed to Washington's half brother Lawrence. He renamed the estate Mount Vernon in honor of Edward Vernon, an admiral in the British Navy under whom he had served. After the death of his father, Washington lived there for a time. After Lawrence's death in 1752, the property came into George Washington's possession.

The estate that he inherited was approximately 2,100 acres (850 hectares) in size, but by the time of his death it had grown to more than 8,000 acres (3,200 hectares). The estate was divided into five separate farms, each under its own management. The farm on which the house sits was known as the Mansion House Farm, but its approximately 500 acres (200 hectares) were developed less as a farm than as a country estate. There were extensive formal gardens, a bowling green, a park flanking the river, and vineyards near one of the gardens.

Tourists visiting Washington's home, Mount Vernon. Brendan Smialowski/ Getty Images

The original house was only a story and a half in height with four small rooms on the main floor. Washington's father erected the foundations of this structure in the late 1730s, but there is evidence of a much older structure dating from the late 17th century. The central portion of the house was probably built in 1743. In anticipation of his marriage in 1759, Washington had the house raised to two and a half stories and began landscaping the surrounding grounds. Extensions on either end of the house were planned in 1773, and work on them continued through the years of the American Revolution. Interior work continued for many more years.

Washington was especially fond of Mount Vernon and felt it was the most "pleasantly situated" estate in the United States. He yearned for a quiet life there but often found himself away on public business. He returned to Mount Vernon in 1797 at the conclusion of his presidency but lived only another two years.

After the death of Martha Washington in 1802, the estate was parceled out to various relatives. By the middle of the 19th century, the Mansion House Farm could no longer support itself. When approached by the Washington heirs, the United States and the Commonwealth of Virginia governments both refused to acquire the property. In 1858 a private group, the Mount Vernon Ladies' Association, raised money to purchase the estate. The association still maintains the site, and the home is open to the public year-round.

Lord Thomas Fairfax, who employed Washington as a land sur-
veyor. Washington earned his first public office, as a county
surveyor, mainly on Fairfax's recommendation. Hulton Archive/
Getty Images

Ferry Farm was left to George's mother, Mary Ball Washington. George's half brother, Lawrence, inherited Epsewasson, and his other half brother, Augustine, inherited Wakefield. Lawrence married Anne Fairfax, a neighbor, and added her adjoining land to the property at Epsewasson. He renamed the estate Mount Vernon, in honor of Adm. Edward Vernon, the British naval officer under whom he served in the West Indies.

After his father's death, George went to live with Augustine at Wakefield and attended Henry William's school, one of the best schools in Virginia. By age 15 George was skilled in mathematics and mapmaking and developed an interest in practical surveying.

In 1748 George went to live with his other half brother, Lawrence, at Mount Vernon. There he met Lord Thomas Fairfax, a cousin of Anne Fairfax. Lord Fairfax owned more than 5 million acres (2 million hectares) in Virginia, and he hired George to help survey his land beyond the Blue Ridge Mountains. Surveying was difficult and dangerous work, but George adapted well and excelled at his new profession. On July 20, 1749, through Lord Fairfax's influence, George Washington was appointed surveyor of Culpeper

County, his first public office. Through his experiences as a surveyor, Washington became more knowledgeable and resourceful about the land, and he gained an enthusiasm for colonizing the West.

FIRST SERVICE AS A MILITARY LEADER

During the years he lived with Lawrence and his family at Mount Vernon, Washington heard many stories of his brother's experiences in the British Navy. These tales inspired Washington to pursue a military career. When Lawrence died in July 1752, Washington inherited Mount Vernon, thus becoming a landowner. In November 1752 Lieutenant Governor Robert Dinwiddie of Virginia appointed Washington adjutant, or assistant, officer for the southern district of Virginia.

The following year, Dinwiddie made Washington a major of an army militia and sent him with a message to the French commander of Fort Le Boeuf (now Waterford, Pa.). The message demanded that the French abandon their forts on the British territory between Lake Ontario and the

Ohio River. Washington delivered the message and returned to Virginia in January 1754 with a full report on the French army's plan to take possession of the Ohio River Valley. After studying Washington's report, Dinwiddie convinced the British government that the French posed a serious threat to the British colonies. Washington's perilous journey had taken 10 weeks, and twice he nearly lost his life. Once, a Native American shot at him from close range; a few days later, Washington was thrown from a raft into an ice-filled stream.

In April 1754 Washington was made lieutenant colonel of the militia. He was ordered to lead nearly 200 troops to take possession of Fort Duquesne, which was located in the Ohio River Valley where the Allegheny and Monongahela rivers meet. The French had a strong hold on Fort Duquesne, and Washington's small militia was unable to overtake the fort. He located an area nearby at Great Meadows (now Confluence, Pa.) and built Fort Necessity for his army. On May 28, 1754, Washington's troops and their Native American allies ambushed and killed or captured all of a French scouting party near Fort

Washington (on horseback) riding into battle as a captain in the American militia during the French and Indian War. SuperStock/ Getty Images

Necessity. The French commander, Coulon de Jumonville, was killed in the attack, and this encounter contributed to the start of the French and Indian War.

The French and Indian War

Washington's skillful maneuvers in the ambush against the French scouting party were recognized by his superior officers, and he was immediately promoted to colonel. He was given command of a small army of Virginia and North Carolina troops and Native American allies. In July 1754 Washington's troops attacked the French forces at Fort Duquesne, but the French and the Native Americans loyal to the French outnumbered them and forced Washington to surrender. The French allowed Washington's army to return to Virginia after he released the French prisoners of war. Despite his defeat, Washington was commended for his valiant efforts against the French by the Virginia House of Burgesses, the representative assembly in colonial Virginia.

Raising the British flag at Fort Duquesne. As commander of all Virginia militia forces, Washington (center) was present at the battle at the fort, which ended the French and Indian War. PhotoQuest/Archive Photos/Getty Images

In February 1755 Washington was sent to serve as aide to British Maj. Gen. Edward Braddock in another offensive against Fort Duquesne. Braddock acknowledged and respected Washington's merit and leadership abilities. He allowed Washington to advise and express his opinions on military strategies. On July 9, 1755, French forces ambushed and defeated Braddock's forces, and Braddock was killed in the battle. Washington displayed initiative and poise as he assembled the remaining troops and led them back to Virginia.

In August 1755 Lieutenant Governor Dinwiddie appointed Washington commander of all Virginia militia forces. Virginia expanded its forces to 1,000 soldiers, and Washington directed the patrols and defense of the entire 400-mile (640-kilometer) western frontier. In 1758 Washington accompanied British Gen. John Forbes and finally defeated the French at Fort Duquesne, which was burned to the ground by the retreating French troops. Forbes established Fort Pitt (now Pittsburgh, Pa.) on the site.

CHAPTER 2

Prerevolutionary Years

While serving in the final campaign against Fort Duquesne, Washington was elected to the Virginia House of Burgesses. Upon the completion of the campaign, he resigned from the army with the honorary rank of brigadier general. He married soon thereafter, and until the eve of the Revolution he devoted himself to his family and to his duties as a large landholder.

MARRIAGE AND FAMILY

On Jan. 6, 1759, Washington married Martha Dandridge, the widow of Daniel Parke Custis. She was a few months older

Portrait of Martha Dandridge Custis, who became Mrs. George Washington. Universal Images Group/Getty Images

than he, was the mother of two children living and two dead, and possessed one of the considerable fortunes of Virginia. Washington had met her the previous March and had asked for her hand before his campaign with Forbes. Though it does not seem to have been a romantic love match, the marriage united two harmonious temperaments and proved happy. Martha was a good housewife, an amiable companion, and a dignified hostess. Like many wellborn women of the era, she had little formal schooling, and Washington often helped her compose important letters.

Some estimates of the property brought to him by this marriage have been exaggerated, but it did include a number of slaves and about 15,000 acres (6,000 hectares), much of it valuable for its proximity to Williamsburg. More important to Washington were the two stepchildren, John Parke ("Jacky") and Martha Parke ("Patsy") Custis, who at the time of the marriage were 6 and 4, respectively. He lavished great affection and care upon them, worried greatly over Jacky's waywardness, and was overcome with grief when Patsy died just before the Revolution. Jacky died during the war, leaving four children. Washington adopted two of Jacky's children, a boy and a girl, and even signed his letters to the boy as "your papa." Himself childless, he thus had a real family.

PLANTATION LIFE

From the time of his marriage, Washington added to the care of Mount Vernon the supervision of the Custis estate on the York River. He minutely inspected operations every day and according to one visitor often

George and Martha Washington posing for a family portrait with Patsy and Jacky Custis, children from Martha's first marriage. Hulton Archive/Getty Images

pulled off his coat and performed ordinary labor. This routine was interrupted by several weeks' attendance every year in the House of Burgesses in Williamsburg. During 1760–74 he was also a justice of the peace for Fairfax County, sitting in court in Alexandria.

In no light does Washington appear more characteristically than as one of the richest, largest, and most industrious of Virginia planters. For six days a week he rose early and worked hard; on Sundays he irregularly attended Pohick Church (16 times in 1760), entertained company, wrote letters, made purchases and sales, and sometimes went fox hunting.

Washington was an innovative farmer. He experimented at breeding cattle, acquired at least one buffalo with the hope of proving its utility as a meat animal, and kept stallions at stud. He also took pride in a peach and apple orchard. He had his own water-powered flour mill, blacksmith shop, brick and charcoal kilns, carpenters, and masons. Coopers, weavers, and his own shoemaker turned out barrels, cotton, linen, woollen goods, and brogans (a type of shoe) for all needs. In short, his estates, in accordance with his orders to overseers to "buy nothing you can make yourselves," were largely

Washington (second right) overseeing activity on his farm. Though busy as a representative in the House of Burgesses, Washington still made time to manage his land, even working alongside his farm hands. MPI/Archive Photos/Getty Images

self-sufficient communities. But he did send large orders to England for farm implements, tools, paint, fine textiles, hardware, and agricultural books and hence was painfully aware of British commercial restrictions.

He meanwhile played a prominent role in the social life of the Tidewater region. The members of the House of Burgesses, a roster of influential Virginians, were all friends. He visited the Byrds of Westover, the Lees of Stratford, the Carters of Shirley

The Washingtons entertaining at Mount Vernon, engaging in a game of cards. SuperStock/Getty Images

and Sabine Hall, and the Lewises of Warner Hall. Mount Vernon often was busy with guests in return. He liked house parties and afternoon tea on the Mount Vernon porch overlooking the grand Potomac; he was fond of picnics, barbecues, and clambakes; and throughout life he enjoyed dancing, frequently going to Alexandria for balls. Cards were a steady diversion, and his accounts record sums lost at them, the largest reaching nearly $16 (£10). His diary sometimes states that in bad weather he was "at home all day, over cards." Billiards was a rival amusement. Not only the theater, when available, but also concerts, cockfights, circuses, puppet shows, and exhibitions of animals received his patronage.

ENTRY INTO POLITICS

After the French and Indian War ended in 1763, Great Britain was in debt as a result of war expenditures. A stronger British military was needed to protect the increased British possessions in the colonies acquired during the war. Parliament, the legislative body of Great Britain's government, implemented several acts aimed at generating revenue from the colonies to alleviate these costs. The Stamp Act of 1765 imposed a tax on newspapers, legal documents, and other business papers. The colonists considered this act an intrusion on their rights, and Great Britain repealed it in 1766. However, Great Britain continued to regulate the colonies in matters of taxation and legislation with the Townshend Acts of 1767, which placed taxes on imported British commodities. In April 1769 Washington presented a plan to the House of Burgesses for boycotting British-made goods.

The Stamp Act

The French and Indian War doubled the debt of the British government and at the same time greatly increased British possessions in America. The British government therefore decided to station British troops in the colonies to prevent the French from recovering Canada and to defend the colonies against the Indians. Most Englishmen thought it only right that the colonies should help pay for the support of these troops. For a partial support of the troops, the British Parliament therefore passed the Stamp Act in 1765. This provided that stamps purchased from the British government should be used on all important documents, periodicals, almanacs, pamphlets, and playing cards.

This tax aroused great opposition among the colonists for three reasons: the colonists thought they should not be taxed except by their own representatives; they opposed the presence of British troops; and the tax had to be paid in silver. This would carry so much of their sound money to England that it would seriously interfere with business.

Many wealthy merchants favored stopping all business that required the use of stamped papers. This, they said, would be perfectly legal, and it would so seriously interfere with the business of British merchants that Parliament would be forced to repeal the law. But printers and lawyers, small shopkeepers and laborers, who would be hurt if business stopped, wanted to disregard the Stamp Act entirely. Both methods of resisting the law were employed to some extent. In general there was a marked interference with business, and the poorer classes suffered greatly in the winter of 1766 for want of employment. The result was that rioting and disturbances were common. This resistance helped to bring about the repeal of the law in March 1766. This step, however, was accompanied by a Declaratory Act setting forth Parliament's supreme power over the colonies in matters of taxation.

Hostilities between the colonists and the British government escalated after the Boston Massacre on March 5, 1770, when British soldiers fired on a group of angry citizens in Boston who were threatening the soldiers. Colonists protested vehemently over British taxation without colonial representation in Parliament. On Dec. 16, 1773, a group of colonists threw 342 chests of tea into Boston Harbor to protest a tea tax. This rebellion, known as the Boston Tea Party, prompted Great Britain to retaliate by passing the Intolerable Acts in 1774. These acts were a series of punitive laws directed against the colonies; among other things, they called for the closing of Boston Harbor and the installation of a military government in Massachusetts. The acts also forced the colonists to provide housing for British troops in colonial dwellings.

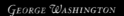

Colonists dumping cargo into the water during what has become known as the Boston Tea Party. This incident was one of several rebellious acts against British rule in the Americas. The Bridgeman Art Library/Getty Images

Washington's political career expanded as dissension grew between the colonists and Great Britain. He believed that the British had attacked the rights of the colonists with

heavy taxes and oppressive laws, and he was ready to defend these rights. In May 1774 Washington and other Virginia legislators signed the resolutions calling for a Continental Congress. He was elected to the Virginia delegation that attended the First Continental Congress in Philadelphia on Sept. 5, 1774. He also attended the Second Continental Congress in 1775.

Many Continental Congress members demanded independence from Great Britain. In April 1775 skirmishes between British troops and the colonists at Lexington and Concord further intensified colonial hostilities toward Great Britain. Washington was not yet in favor of independence, but he was prepared to support armed resistance against British authority throughout the colonies.

CHAPTER 3

Revolutionary Leadership

Recognizing Washington's military experience and leadership, the Continental Congress made him commander in chief of all colonial military forces in June 1775. At once he showed characteristic decision and energy in organizing volunteers, collecting provisions and munitions, and rallying Congress and the colonies to his support. In the ensuing American Revolution, he proved a brilliant commander and a stalwart leader, despite several defeats.

HEAD OF THE COLONIAL FORCES

As commander in chief, Washington asked for no pay beyond his actual expenses

Washington being named commander in chief of colonial military forces during the Continental Congress of 1775. **Library of Congress Prints and Photographs**

because he considered the assignment his duty to protect the rights and values of the citizens whom he served. Reports of how courageously the colonial militia fought against British soldiers at Bunker Hill in June

Washington (center, on horseback) *during the siege of Boston in March 1776, which resulted in British forces retreating from the city.* **Interim Archives/Archive Photos/Getty Images**

1775 gave him confidence about the impending war. However, he faced many hardships as he assembled the Continental Army. His recruits were untrained and poorly paid,

terms of army enlistment were short, and his officers frequently quarreled among themselves. Washington persevered to build his army into trained soldiers equipped with adequate supplies.

Washington commanded the respect of his troops through his confidence, poise, and determination as a general. In March 1776 his army staged a siege and eventually expelled British troops from Boston. Washington also instilled a sense of national pride in his troops. He maintained discipline within his army by punishing dishonest soldiers and deserters. At the same time, he attended to their welfare by petitioning to the Continental Congress for better rations and pay.

BATTLES IN THE NORTH

On July 4, 1776, the Continental Congress adopted the Declaration of Independence for the 13 colonies. Congress wrote the Articles of Confederation, the first constitution in the United States, to implement a national government.

Iconic image of Washington crossing the Delaware River, by Emanuel Gottlieb Leutze. © SuperStock

In December 1776 Washington's forces crossed the Delaware River from Pennsylvania to New Jersey and won battles at Trenton and Princeton. The Continental

Army gained an advantage in the war with Gen. Horatio Gates's victory in New York at the Battle of Saratoga in October 1777. However, Washington's army suffered losses against the British forces in Pennsylvania at the battles of Brandywine and Germantown in the fall of 1777. In December 1777 Washington withdrew to Valley Forge, Pa., where he set up winter quarters and reorganized his army despite the bitter cold.

By 1778 France recognized the United States as an independent nation and sent military support to help Washington's forces fight the British. In July 1778 a French naval fleet blockaded the British troops in New York City, leaving the British isolated from reinforcements. After

Winter at Valley Forge

An area about 22 miles (35 kilometers) northwest of Philadelphia, Pa., Valley Forge served as the headquarters of Gen. George Washington and the encampment of the Continental Army in the winter of 1777–78, during the American Revolution. The major portions of the original camp are now part of Valley Forge National Historical Park, along the Schuylkill River in southeastern Pennsylvania. The 3,465-acre (1,402-hectare) park

Washington's troops shown hunkering down at Valley Forge during the brutal winter of 1777. PhotoQuest/Archive Photos/ Getty Images

includes Washington's headquarters, re-creations of log buildings, fortifications, and a memorial arch.

The Continental Army of about 11,000 encamped there in December 1777 after the battles of Brandywine and Germantown. The site was chosen partly because of its strategic location between the British army in Philadelphia and the Continental Congress, which was temporarily quartered in York, Pa. Thousands of soldiers were barefoot and without adequate clothing in the bitter cold. Many died of exposure, and more than 2,000 deserted. Horses starved to death. Congress was unable to provide help despite Washington's pleas in this darkest period of the Revolutionary War. Yet the troops did not lose their courage or morale. Under Baron Frederick William von Steuben, the soldiers received instruction in military drill. When spring came, the troops emerged as a well-disciplined and efficient fighting force.

1779 the theater of war shifted to the South with major battles in Charleston, S.C., and Richmond, Va.

CONCLUSION OF THE WAR

The final decisive stroke of the war, the capture of Gen. Charles Cornwallis, the commander of the British Army, during a siege at Yorktown, Va., is to be credited chiefly to Washington's vision. With the domestic situation intensely gloomy early in 1781, he was hampered by the feebleness of Congress and by popular discouragement. A French army had arrived to reinforce him in 1780, and Washington had pressed the French admiral comte de Grasse to assist in an attack upon either Cornwallis in the south or Sir Henry Clinton in New York. In Aug. the French admiral sent definite word that he preferred the Chesapeake, with its large area and deep water, as the scene of his operations. Within a week, on Aug. 19, 1781, Washington marched south with his army, leaving Gen. William Heath with 4,000 men to hold West Point.

Washington hurried his troops through New Jersey, embarked them on transports in Delaware Bay, and landed them at Williamsburg, where he had arrived on September 14. Cornwallis had retreated to Yorktown and entrenched his army of 7,000 British regulars. Their works were completely invested before the end of the month; the siege was pressed with vigor by the allied armies under Washington, consisting of 5,500 Continentals, 3,500 Virginia militia, and 5,000 French regulars. On October 19,

Artist's depiction of the surrender of British general Cornwallis at Yorktown. Military strategy conceived by Washington (center, left) made this final victory possible. Library of Congress Prints and Photographs

Cornwallis surrendered. By this campaign, probably the finest single display of Washington's generalship, the war was brought to a virtual close.

LIFE AFTER THE REVOLUTION

The Treaty of Paris was signed on Sept. 3, 1783, officially ending the American Revolution. Washington remained with the Continental Congress until December 1783, when he resigned his commission and returned to his home at Mount Vernon. There his farms continued to thrive. He recognized the Potomac River as a great

waterway for settlers and trade goods, and he predicted that western territories such as Kentucky, Tennessee, and Ohio would become states. Washington himself acquired more than 50,000 acres (20,234 hectares) in the western territories.

General George Washington resigning his military commission during a meeting of the Continental Congress in 1783. Universal Images Group/Getty Images

Washington was chosen to preside over the Constitutional Convention of 1787 in Philadelphia. Under the Articles of Confederation, the United States government was incapable of governing the

Painting by Junius Brutus Stearns showing Washington addressing the members of the Constitutional Convention in Philadelphia, 1787. SuperStock/Getty Images

instabilities that existed within the states. By July 1788 a new constitution had been drafted and 11 of the 13 states ratified the United States Constitution. By 1790 the remaining two states, North Carolina and Rhode Island, had also ratified the Constitution, and Congress became the governing body of the United States government.

CHAPTER 4

Presidency

On Feb. 4, 1789, the electors granted all 69 electoral votes to George Washington, thereby unanimously electing him as president of the United States. John Adams was elected vice president. Washington was inaugurated into office on April 30, 1789. His presidency was to be a time of adjustment to a new type of government for the people of the United States.

WASHINGTON'S ADMINISTRATION

The newly formed United States government consisted of a legislative branch, the Congress; a judicial branch, the Supreme Court; and an executive branch, which was

Illustration capturing the moment Washington took the oath
of office as president of the United States of America.
© SuperStock

headed by Washington and included his Cabinet. The first Cabinet members included Thomas Jefferson as secretary of state, Henry Knox as secretary of war, Edmund Randolph as attorney general, and Alexander Hamilton as secretary of the treasury. In 1790 Washington approved a permanent location for the United States capital on the Potomac River. The capital was moved from New York City to Philadelphia until the new capital was established.

During Washington's administration, the authority of the federal government was greatly strengthened. Washington and Hamilton chartered the Bank of the United States in 1791, and the federal government assumed responsibility for both national and state debts. Taxes were placed on imported goods and certain private property within the states, and money was deposited into the national treasury for paying debts. Also in 1791 the states ratified the Bill of Rights, the first 10 amendments to the Constitution, which granted United States citizens their basic rights.

Washington was reelected to a second term as president in 1792, with Adams again serving as his vice president. Three new states were admitted to the United States

Members of Washington's first cabinet, including (left to right) Secretary of War Henry Knox, Secretary of State Thomas Jefferson, Attorney General Edmund Randolph, Treasury Secretary Alexander Hamilton, and Washington. FPG/Archive Photos/Getty Images

during Washington's administration— Vermont in 1791, Kentucky in 1792, and Tennessee in 1796.

When war broke out between France and Great Britain in 1793, Washington decided that the United States should remain neutral in foreign affairs. Even though the United States owed France a debt for assistance in the American Revolution and promised to help France in any future conflicts, Washington felt that the United States was not prepared to enter another war so soon. Accordingly, he issued the Proclamation of Neutrality in April 1793, which stated that the United States must maintain a sense of national identity, independent from any other country's influence. Several future presidents, including James Monroe, followed Washington's neutrality policy.

POLITICAL PARTIES

National political parties emerged as a result of Washington's foreign policies. Washington and Hamilton were opposed to the segregation of the government that political parties created. Hamilton, however, led the Federalist party with Adams to support

The First "First Lady"

As wife of the first president of the United States, Martha Washington had no examples to follow in her position as First Lady when George Washington took office in 1789. Although she was reluctant to assume a public role, her willingness to do so contributed to the eventual strength and influence of the position of First Lady.

In 1789, shortly after her husband's inauguration as president, Martha joined him in New York City, then the national capital. She became known to Americans as "Lady Washington" and established the precedent of First Lady as hostess for presidential receptions and other social functions. The couple's rented home on Broadway also served as the president's office, exposing Martha to her husband's callers and drawing her into political discussions more than would have been the case had home and office been separated.

When Philadelphia became the seat of government in 1790 and the Washingtons moved to a house on High Street, Martha's hospitality became even more elaborate. The First Lady took no stands on public issues, but she was criticized by some for entertaining on a scale too opulent for a republican government. The Washingtons, however, felt some lavishness was necessary to help the new republic be accepted as the equal of the established governments of Europe. The couple also had rather informal receptions called "drawing rooms" every Friday.

The Washingtons happily retired to Mount Vernon in 1797 after completion of the president's second term of office, and Martha continued to reside there following her husband's death in 1799. She burned all of their letters to one another in an effort to ensure lasting privacy. Martha died following a severe fever on May 22, 1802, at Mount Vernon and was buried beside Washington in a family tomb on the estate.

Portrait of First Lady Martha Washington. Photo Researchers/ Getty Images

their policies. James Madison and Thomas Jefferson founded the Republican Party. The Federalists advocated a strong central government and wanted to maintain close ties with Great Britain. The Republicans were opposed to the authority of a strong national government that decreased the power of state and local governments. Republicans also wanted to preserve their old alliance with France. Washington favored the Federalist ideals of government but worked to sustain a balance between the two parties.

CHALLENGES AND BOUNDARY DISPUTES

The United States government met its first serious domestic challenge with the Whiskey Rebellion in July 1794. Washington set a tax on whiskey to help pay the national debt. Farmers in western Pennsylvania who relied on the income from selling whiskey were outraged by the tax. These farmers resisted the tax by assaulting federal revenue officers. After negotiations between the federal government and the farmers failed, Washington dispatched local state

Citizens of Pennsylvania assaulting a federal tax collector using tar and feathers during the episode known as the Whiskey Rebellion. Kean Collection/Archive Photos/Getty Images

militias and federal troops to quell the rebellion. The national government prevailed over a rebellious adversary and won the support of state governments in enforcing federal law within the states.

Washington's administration faced boundary disputes with the Native Americans on the western frontier, Great Britain in the northeast and northwest, and Spain in the south. Settlers in the Ohio River Valley fought Native Americans over claims on the western frontier boundaries. Washington dispatched an army under the command of Gen. Anthony Wayne to defend the settlements from the Native Americans. Wayne built a chain of forts from Ohio to Indiana to protect the settlements. He finally defeated the Native Americans at the battle of Fallen Timbers on Aug. 20, 1794.

Washington authorized John Jay, chief justice of the Supreme Court, to negotiate boundary disputes with Great Britain. In the Jay Treaty, signed on Nov. 19, 1794, Great Britain and the United States negotiated the boundaries between the United States and British North America. Great Britain also granted the United States trading privileges with England and the British East Indies.

John Jay, author of the Jay Treaty, which settled boundary disputes between the United States and Great Britain. **Library of Congress Prints and Photographs**

Thomas Pinckney, an American diplomat, was sent to Spain for negotiations concerning U.S. interests in Spanish-owned territories. Pinckney's Treaty, signed on Oct. 27, 1795, established the southern boundary of the United States at 31° N. latitude, opened the Mississippi River to U.S. trade through Spanish territories, and granted Americans a tax-free port in New Orleans.

From 1794 to 1798 the Barbary pirates of North Africa attacked U.S. merchant ships in the Atlantic. The Continental Navy, created in 1775 and disbanded in 1784, was restored in 1794 to protect U.S. vessels. Washington signed the Navy's first commission to John Barry, who was made captain of the frigate *United States*. In April 1798 Congress created the Department of the Navy.

FINAL DAYS IN OFFICE

When Washington's second term ended in 1796, he refused to run for a third term. Washington's Farewell Address was first published in the *American Daily Advertiser*, a Philadelphia newspaper, on Sept. 19, 1796. It gave the people of the United States his reasons for not accepting a third term in office. He considered it

**Letter appointing John Barry captain of the frigate United
States.** *Barry has the honor of being the first commissioned officer in the United States Navy.* © AP Images

unwise for one person to hold such a powerful
position for so long. All successive U.S. presidents served no more than two terms except
Franklin D. Roosevelt, who was elected to four
terms. In 1951 the 22nd Amendment to the
Constitution was ratified, stating, "No person
shall be elected to the office of the President
more than twice...." On March 4, 1797,

John Adams was sworn in as president with Thomas Jefferson as his vice president.

RETIREMENT

Washington retired to Mount Vernon, where he spent time with his family and resumed the management of his farms and estates. In 1798 an expectation of war with France caused President John Adams to appoint Washington commander in chief of a provisional army. The threat of war diminished, however, and Washington never took command.

Washington riding his horse around the grounds of his estate and farm. MPI/Archive Photos/Getty Images

A colorized image of Washington's tomb on the grounds of Mount Vernon. Curt Teich Postcard Archives/Archive Photos/ Getty Images

On Dec. 12, 1799, Washington returned home from a horseback ride through his farms in cold, snowy weather. He developed laryngitis and became weak and ill. He died two days later, on Dec. 14, 1799, in his Mount Vernon home and was buried in the family vault at Mount Vernon. John Marshall, who served Washington at Valley Forge, quoted part of a eulogy for Washington by the American Revolutionary officer Henry "Light-Horse Harry" Lee. The quote exemplified Washington's place in United States history: "First in war, first in peace, and first in the hearts of his countrymen."

CONCLUSION

In 1800 the United States capital was moved from Philadelphia to the newly developed city of Washington, D.C., named in honor of George Washington. The city is on the Potomac River in an area once part of Maryland and Virginia. George Washington had helped design the layout of the city while in office. In 1853 Congress created the Washington Territory, which became a state in 1889, and named it in memory of the nation's first president. Thirty-two counties in various states were later named commemorating George Washington. The Washington Monument, in Washington, D.C., is yet another lasting tribute to the man considered by most Americans to be the Father of Their Country.

Glossary

amendment A proposed change to a country's constitution.

dissension A particularly strong or violent disagreement.

embark To go onboard a ship or land vehicle for transportation.

eulogy Spoken or written praise in honor of someone who has died.

Federalist A member of a major political party in the early years of the United States favoring a strong centralized national government.

frigate A three-masted, fully rigged sailing ship, with weapons carried on a single gun deck and additional guns on the poop and forecastle.

hostilities Conflict with or resistance to another person or group.

innovative Regarding a new, clever, and creative item or idea.

kiln An oven or furnace used to produce a substance (such as pottery) by heat and fire.

militia A body of citizens banded together in military service.

munitions A stockpile of ammunition and weapons.

neutrality Taking a stance of not favoring one party or another.

patronage Lending support, using wealth or influence, to help an individual, an institution, or a cause.

plantation An agricultural estate usually worked by resident labor.

preeminent Having the highest rank or the most dignity or importance.

provisions A stock of needed materials or supplies, typically including food.

ratification The act of approving and formally authorizing something, usually some form of legislation.

regulate To bring under the control of law or constituted authority.

siege A military blockade of a city or fortified place to compel it to surrender.

surveyor One whose job is to examine an item, notably land, to determine its condition and value.

For More Information

American Revolution Association
306 Hampton Park
Camden, SC 29021
(801) 549-6710
Web site: http://www.
americanrevolutionassociation.com
The American Revolution Association is a
nonprofit organization that promotes
and preserves the historic significance of
important people, places, and events of
the American Revolution. The association offers education, publications, and
assistance with historic-site preservation.

Canadian Historical Association (CHA)
501-130 Albert Street
Ottawa, ON K1P 5G4
Canada
(613) 233-7885
Web site: http://www.cha-shc.ca

The CHA promotes research and scholarship of national history, including the Quebec Act and American Revolutionary battles fought on Canadian soil. The association accomplishes its goals through publications, lobbying efforts, and various other endeavors.

George Washington Foundation
1201 Washington Avenue
Fredericksburg, VA 22401
(540) 373-3381
Web site: http://www.kenmore.org
The George Washington Foundation is dedicated to the preservation of Washington's boyhood home and his sister's nearby plantation. By offering tours, educational programs, and special events, the foundation seeks to honor the legacy of America's first president.

Historic Mount Vernon
3200 Mount Vernon Memorial Highway
Alexandria, VA 22121
(703) 780-2000
Web site: http://www.mountvernon.org
Visitors to Mount Vernon can tour George Washington's historic home and learn all

about his life through the exhibits and artifacts displayed at the Museum and Education Center. Washington's estate also includes his extensive plantation, which features a blacksmith and green-house as well as restored slave quarters, among other sites.

Miller Center
2201 Old Ivy Road
Charlottesville, VA 22904
(434) 924-7236
Web site: http://millercenter.org
The Miller Center at the University of Virginia furthers understanding of all aspects of the presidency, political history, and policy through its various research initiatives, programs, events, and fellowship opportunities.

National Museum of American History (NMAH)
14th Street and Constitution Avenue NW
Washington, DC 20002
(202) 633-1000
Web site: http://americanhistory.si.edu
The NMAH is dedicated to promoting public interest in the events that shaped

the American nation. Its The American Presidency: A Glorious Burden exhibit profiles American presidents through collections of their belongings.

Organization of American Historians (OAH)
112 North Bryan Avenue
Bloomington, IN 47408
(812) 855-7311
Web site: http://www.oah.org
Committed to advancing scholarship in the field of American history, the OAH supports a number of programs, publications, and resources for students, teachers, researchers, and professionals in the field.

WEB SITES

Due to the changing nature of Internet links, Rosen Educational Services has developed an online list of Web sites related to the subject of this book. This site is updated regularly. Please use this link to access the list:

http://www.rosenlinks.com/pppl/geowa

For Further Reading

Adler, David A. *George Washington: An Illustrated Biography* (Holiday House, 2004).

Brady, Patricia. *Martha Washington: An American Life* (Viking, 2005).

Burns, James MacGregor, and Dunn, Susan. *George Washington* (Times Books, 2004).

Collard, Sneed B. *George Washington, Our First President* (Marshall Cavendish Benchmark, 2010).

Collier, Christopher, and Collier, James Lincoln. *The American Revolution, 1763–1783* (Benchmark Books, 1998).

Fontes, Justine, and Fontes, Ron. *George Washington: Soldier, Hero, President* (Dorling Kindersley, 2001).

Fradin, Dennis B. *The Battle of Yorktown* (Marshall Cavendish Benchmark, 2009).

Freedman, Russell. *Washington at Valley Forge* (Holiday House, 2008).

Harness, Cheryl. *George Washington* (National Geographic, 2006).

Keller, Kristin Thoennes. *George Washington* (Bridgestone Books, 2002).

Murphy, Jim. *The Crossing: How George Washington Saved the American Revolution* (Scholastic Press, 2010).

Nardo, Don. *The American Revolution* (Greenhaven Press, 1998).

Santella, Andrew. *Mount Vernon* (Compass Point Books, 2005).

Schanzer, Rosalyn. *George vs. George: The American Revolution as Seen from Both Sides* (National Geographic, 2004).

Smith, Richard Norton. *Patriarch: George Washington and the New American Nation* (Houghton Mifflin, 1993).

Index